GW01418181

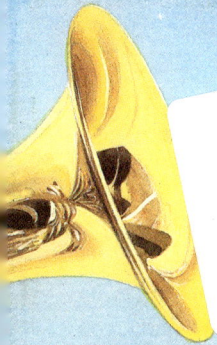

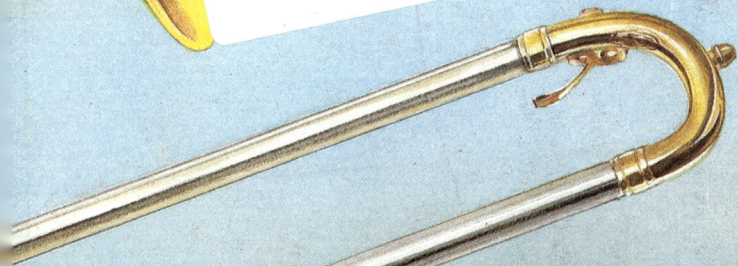

Written by Genevieve Laurencin
Illustrated by Claude and Denise Millet

Translated by Margaret Malpas, B.Lit, M.A.,
who is a teacher of music

ISBN 1 85103 063 8
First published 1989 in the United Kingdom
by Moonlight Publishing Ltd
131 Kensington Church Street, London W8
© 1988 by Editions Gallimard

English text © 1989 by Moonlight Publishing Ltd
Typeset in Great Britain by Saxon Ltd, Derby
Printed in Italy by La Editoriale Libraria

POCKET • WORLDS

The Making of Music

The world is full of music . . .

Listen. . . Leaves rustle, birds sing, insects buzz, the waterfall roars, thunder booms, an aircraft drones across the sky. You can make all sorts of different noises too. You can sing or shout or whistle, clap your hands or stamp your feet. You can rap on a box, blow down a pipe, twang on a bow, rattle a tin can. Try blowing on a blade of grass held between your thumbs – can you make it screech? Or blow gently into an empty bottle to make an eerie, echoing wail. When you do any of these things, you are making your very own musical instrument.

There are three big families of musical instruments: **percussion**, which you hit; **strings**, which you draw a bow across; and **wind**, which you blow through.

Have you ever played a xylophone?

The xylophone is a percussion instrument, because you hit it to make a sound. Each bar gives a different note, so that you can play a scale, or a tune.

Not all percussion instruments can play tunes. Some, like the side drum and the big bass drum, just make a loud noise; the triangle can play only one note.

17th century kettle-drums. The skins on the tops of these drums could be made tighter or looser to give different notes.

The earliest music-makers played <u>percussion instruments.</u>

Side drum, triangle, cymbals, bass drum, gong, vibraphone:
all these are members of the percussion family.

These first instruments were mostly used just to beat out a steady rhythm, but nowadays people use percussion to make interesting new sounds.

You can make different sounds by hitting the instruments with different sticks: hard wooden ones or padded ones, metal ones or wire brushes. Or you can just use your hands.

Maracas to shake, claves to knock together, a guiro to scrape, castanets to click: these instruments come from Spain and South America, and you might see them used in the orchestra if you go to a concert.

All over the world, people play percussion instruments.

Musicians in Burundi, in **Central Africa**, play their drums at the festival to celebrate the annual seed-sowing. After the great day, the drums are silent until the next year's festival.

People in Mali and Guinea dance to the music of these wooden xylophones.

The Ko drum is used in the theatre in **China**; the different rhythms played on it help the audience to understand the play.

Japanese Kodos are athletes as well as musicians. They have to fight an enormous drum, to free the gods and goddesses who are shut up inside. If the Kodos can hit the drum hard enough, the prisoners escape, and bring rain and sunshine to the earth.

The best-known instrument in the string family is the violin.

You play it by drawing a bow across the strings to make them vibrate.

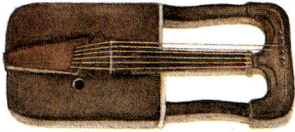

The crwth was played with a bow long ago in Wales.

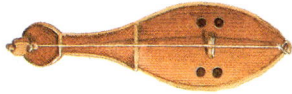

Minstrels in the Middle Ages played the rebeck.

Before the first violins were made, in the middle of the 16th century, people played the viol. Most viols were held up on the musician's arm, almost like a violin, but the viola da gamba (the name means 'leg viol') rested between the player's knees, rather like a 'cello. At first, viols were used for serious music, and the violin, or fiddle, was only considered suitable for dance-tunes; but now the violin leads the orchestra.

Viola da gamba

When you see a violin in pieces like this, it looks easy to fit together. **But it takes an enormous amount of time, skill and patience to make a violin.** First the craftsman has to cut out, shape, glue, drill, smooth and varnish more than 70 pieces of special woods. Then he puts on the four strings. The hair which the bowmaker fixes to the stick of the bow is taken from the tails of white stallions found in Canada or Siberia. Ordinary horse-hair is not long enough.

Stradivari (1644-1737), who lived at Cremona in Italy, made the finest violins in the world. They now sell for a fortune.

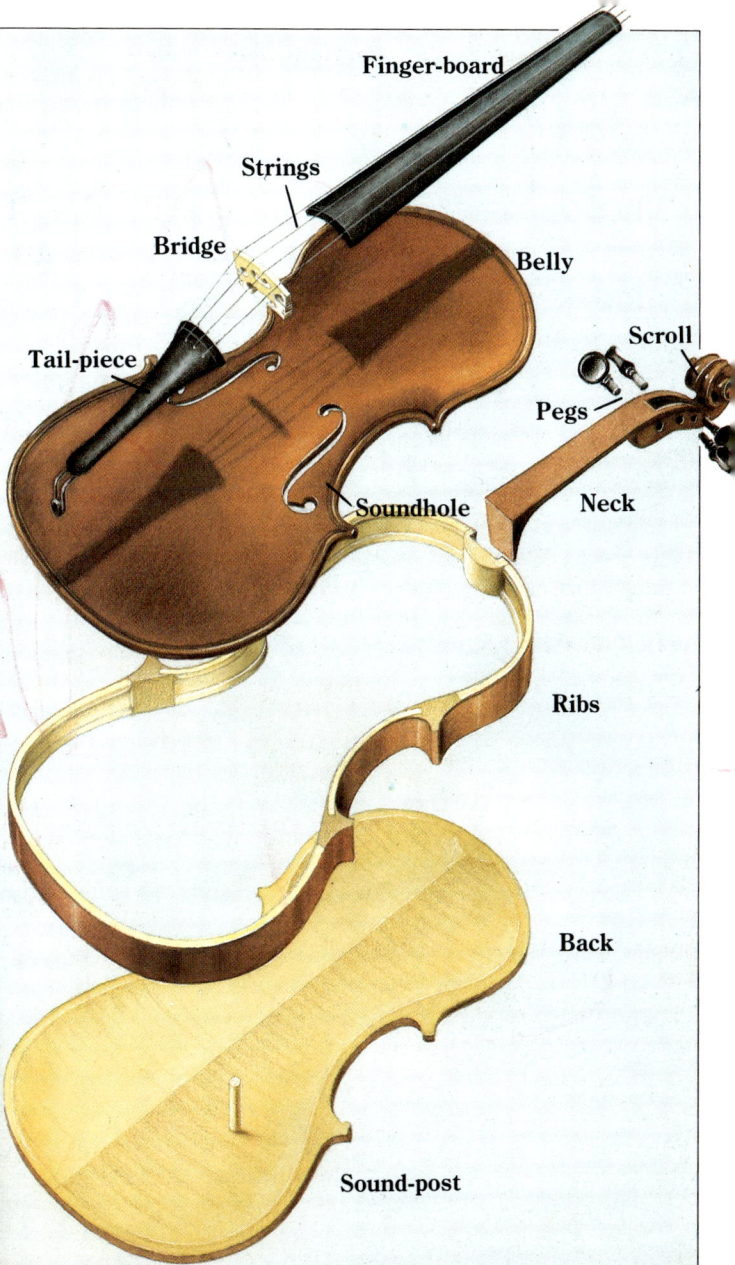

Finger-board

Strings

Bridge

Belly

Scroll

Pegs

Tail-piece

Neck

Soundhole

Ribs

Back

Sound-post

The harp has 46 strings, but it does not belong to the string family because you pluck it with your fingers instead of using a bow.

The string family:

Violin **Viola** **'Cello** **Double bass**

Since the eighteenth century, many composers have written pieces for the string quartet: two violins, a viola and a 'cello.

High and low

A thick string plays a deeper note than a thin string; a long string plays a deeper note than a short string. A double bass can rumble like thunder; a violin, which has shorter and thinner strings, plays much higher notes.

Dancing-masters used to have tiny violins, called 'kits', which they could carry around in a pocket.

All you need to make a wind instrument is a tube you can blow through.
In prehistoric times, people made flutes from animal bones.

This bone flute is about 3,000 years old.

Pan-pipes were first made of reeds tied together. Each reed is a different length and cut diagonally at the end. You blow across the tops of the pipes.

Later, people in China tied together lengths of bamboo to make pan-pipes. Each pipe plays a different note: the shortest one gives the highest note, the largest one the lowest.

There are two kinds of wind instruments:
woodwind and brass.

Minstrels in the Middle Ages played the sackbut, a brass instrument like a trombone, and the wooden chalumeau, an early version of the clarinet.

Listen to the band!

Have you ever been to a carnival, and heard the brass band playing loud, rousing music to make everyone feel cheerful?

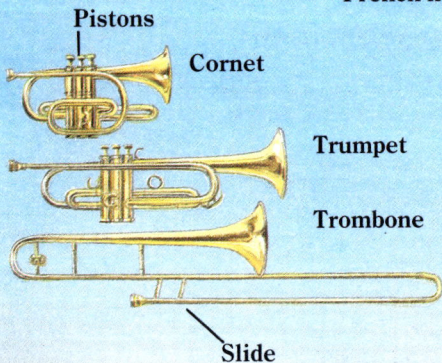

French horn

Pistons

Cornet

Trumpet

Trombone

Slide

A brass band in Louisiana

When you play a brass instrument, you can make a higher note by tightening your lips. The pistons, and the slide of the trombone, make the tube longer or shorter. By using your lips and changing the length of the tube, you can play every note.

Tuba

This is what the inside of a recorder looks like. You blow through the narrow part on the left of the picture.

Woodwind instruments are not always made of wood. Sometimes flutes are made of silver. But all the woodwind are tubes with holes in them. You play a note by making the air vibrate inside the tube.

You hold a flute sideways and blow across the mouthpiece.

Try playing a recorder. Put your fingers over the holes nearest the mouthpiece, and you will make a high note; cover the other holes as well, one by one, and you will play down the scale. The longer the tube, the lower the note.

Piccolo

Oboe

Clarinet

Bassoon

Upright piano

By the time he was six, Mozart was already a famous pianist and beginning to write his own music. When he composed music he called it 'looking for notes which love each other'.

Grand piano. A full-size concert grand is 2.75 m long.

Have you tried making music on the piano? You can make it play in all sorts of ways – soft and gentle, bright and ringing, or loud and thunderous – just by the way your fingers touch the keys.

How does it work? Inside the piano are hammers covered in felt, and strings of different lengths; when you press the key, a hammer hits the string to play the note. The pedals make the sounds last a longer or a shorter time. A piano has all the notes of the scale seven times over.

The orchestra is like one big, magical instrument. Strings and woodwind, brass and percussion play separately or all together.

Side drum

Xylophone

Bass drum

French horns

Trumpets

Harp

Flutes

Oboes

First violins

Second violin

This is how the orchestra is arranged.
Each musician has a special place.

The conductor beats time to help the musicians play together, and tells them how he thinks the music should be played.

Triangle

Cymbals

Kettle-drums

Tubas

Trombones

Clarinets

Bassoons

Double basses

Violas

'Cellos

Conductor

Orchestras in other countries are very different from ours.

The Gagaku orchestra in Japan uses very ancient instruments. In the front row there are koto zithers; people say the sound of the koto is like a dragon on a beach talking to the sea.

Gamelan

On the island of Bali, the people sing, dance and perform shadow-plays to the music of an orchestra called a gamelan. Music is very popular on Bali – there are said to be more than 2,000 gamelans on the island!

Tabla   Tambura   Sitar

This Indian trio is a very small orchestra: a pair of drums, called the tabla, and two types of lute: the sitar and the tambura. Playing the tabla may look easy, but in fact it takes years to learn all the complicated rhythms. Often the musician plays two different rhythms at once, one on each drum.

Jazz began in Louisiana, in the southern United States, when people started to play African music on Western instruments. Jazz is not written down; instead, the musicians start with a basic tune and then make up their own music around it. This is called improvisation.

The main instrument in most rock bands is the electric guitar.

New sounds, new kinds of music. Nowadays, there are computers which can make sounds like traditional instruments, or make a completely new sort of electronic music.

Weird and wonderful

All sorts of extraordinary instruments have been invented through the centuries, as musicians tried to improve upon traditional instruments. A few, like Sax's saxophone, have been successful, but many have disappeared.

The serpent, invented in France in the seventeenth century, had to be this shape so that the player could reach all the finger-holes. It was made of leather-covered wood.

This 19th-century tenor trombone had seven tubes and six pistons, instead of one tube and a slide. It must have made a lot of noise!

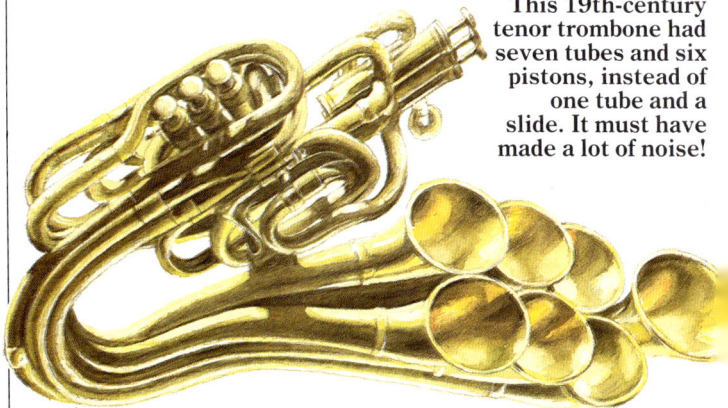

The harp-lyre, invented in 1827, was neither a harp nor a lyre; it was a guitar, with 3 sets of strings and 3 necks.

Modern composers use all sorts of sounds in their music: a typewriter, or clanking chains, or cowbells. In one piece, the orchestra does not play at all – the music comes from the audience as they cough and shuffle their feet!

This modern percussion instrument was meant not so much for playing and listening to as for looking at! It was invented by the French artists, the Bachet brothers.

Index

Some music on record that you will enjoy:
Peter and the Wolf (Prokofiev)
A Young Person's Guide to the Orchestra (Britten)
Carnival of the Animals (Saint-Saëns)
Fireworks Music and *Water Music* (Handel)
Eine Kleine Nachtmusik (Mozart)